I dedicate this to Jehovah, the God of my vision and the Creator of me, in His own image to be a vessel for the Kingdom.

I dedicate this to my parents, Dr. Carolyn and Nolan Davis, my brothers, Nolan Jay and Sean Thomas, my nephew, Moochie and my nieces, Mabba and Ms. Tootie.

I dedicate these 100 personal jewels to all of my aspiring artists, performers, creatives, curators, writers, and musicians who continue to seek honesty and truth about the business of entertainment.

DISCLAIMER: The opinions and views expressed within this book solely belong to author and not authors' affiliates and/or management. Always seek professional council when engaging in any lawful and binding agreements.

#ATD100

Memorize, become familiar and know the keys of your favorite songs. When signing up for an open mic, per se, musicians like it when you know what song you'd like to perform, plus the key you're comfortable performing the song.

99

Be versed in all musical genres.

98

Professionally download sheet music to your favorite songs for any and all auditions. Unless the audition states 'a cappella,' it looks professional when presenting sheet music. Visit www.musicnotes.com!

When completing a W4, its safest to input '0' for all blank spaces. When doing so, the employer will withhold the maximum number of taxes. This will save you from owing in back taxes. Better safe than sorry.

96

Talking back to a Director of

any project is a #negative.

95

READ EVERY AGREEMENT, EVERY CONTRACT. Can't afford one? Try contacting a college/university and partner with them to utilize one of their students to assist you on clauses that you may or may not understand.

94

Gag Order means "a judge's order that a case may not be discussed in public." #ijs

93

Performance Rights Organizations, aka PROs, are responsible for tracking and collecting performance royalties generated from terrestrial and internet radio. In the US, they are ASCAP, BMI, SESAC.

92

All singers should consider acting/musical theatre.

When booking a show, introduce yourself immediately to your house and stage engineers. They can be your best friend or worst enemy as it pertains to your live performance.

$ave. $ave. $ave your money. Have an audition out-of-town? Submitting via video is cool. But being in the actual room with the casting directors is always a bonus. Get that plane ticket. Sleep on someone's couch. But $ave up to be in that room.

89

For the sake of reporting on your taxes, track your miles with www.mileiq.com. It is one of the best app's ever. Thank me later.

You're the "new kid on the block" when you book a show. Listen and observe your surroundings for approximately a month. You will be surprised how much you learn what "to do" *AND* what "not to do" during the duration of your *new* job/opportunity.

Everyone is NOT your friend. Choose wisely. Some of your castmates are merely cubicle, co-workers. Not your "at-home, in-your-personal-space-wine-buddies."

86

Create a repertoire of songs. And update it monthly, if possible.

85

Often times, stage managers are

paid higher salaries than actors.

Explore your gifts wisely.

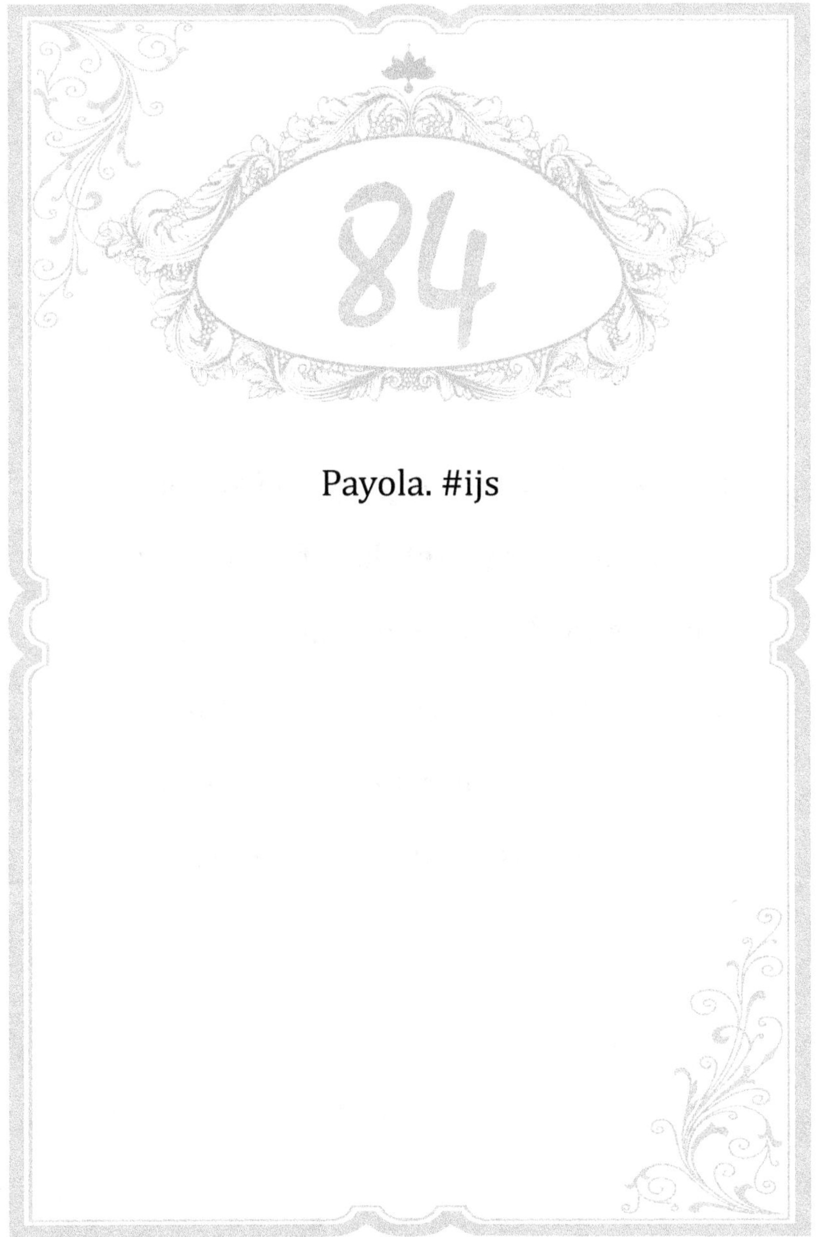

84

Payola. #ijs

83

If performing a gig and you have original music in the marketplace for purchase, innovatively create mashups of cover tunes and your music. It will allow your audience to hear a familiar song while being introduced to your music.

82

If you are cast as an understudy, you betta be on point come showtime.

Verbal commitments can happen quickly. To safely cover your footsteps, immediately send an email and start off by writing, "Per our conversation..." Some people are quick to get amnesia.

80

www.Songsplits.com is a web-based version of a written song splits sheet. It is a songwriter-focused platform that captures, verifies, and manages song split information directly from songwriters and all those involved in the composition.

When completing a song splits sheet
and registering a song with your PRO,
it's an excellent idea to gather all
Interested Parties Information, also
known as the IPI#: a 9- digit number
used to uniquely identify a songwriter
or publisher. Rights holders are assigned
IPI numbers when they are granted
membership to a PRO. Your IPI number
is not the same as your PRO member ID.

78

First Step after writing a song:

Copyright it via www.copyright.gov.

360 Deals are exclusive recording artist contracts that allow a record label to receive a percentage of the earnings from ALL of an artists' activities. Not just on album sales.

Under this type of contract, introduced in 2002, the label will collect a percentage of multiple revenue streams, such as publishing royalties, live concert fees, merchandise sales, endorsement deals, book and/or movie deals, ringtones, AND your weekly "hustle" gigs.

If you are a self-employed artist/musician, and you receive 1099's, roughly set aside 1/3 of your income in a savings or under your bed and pay them when the IRS starts knocking. Or be one step ahead of the IRS and pay them quarterly.*

Answering *some* phone calls before a show sometimes brings bad energy. Give yourself 30:00 minutes of quiet and ease of mind before walking on that stage.

74

Invest in a professionally tangible and visual EPK (Electronic Press Kit).*

Mechanical Royalties are a royalty paid to a songwriter whenever a copy of one of their songs is made. For instance, when a record label presses a CD of your song, you are due a mechanical royalty. Mechanical royalties are paid by whoever obtains a mechanical license to reproduce and distribute a piece of music, such as in album form or as ringtone, digital download, or interactive stream. In the U.S., the Harry Fox Agency is the group that issues mechanical licenses and collects royalties to pay out to the rights holders. PLEASE NOTE: There are various ways of dealing with mechanical royalties AND they differ from country to country.*

72

To collect mechanical royalties, you will need to become a publisher affiliate at Harry Fox Agency. If you're on your own, you must have a commercially distributed record release in the US within the last year. Don't forget your international royalties.*

DO NOT handle business via text message. If someone wants to communicate with you about booking you or requesting your services, simply respond by saying, "I am not at liberty to handle business via text message. Please contact someone from my team at..." This message will always show you if people are on the up and up.

70

Having an @domain.com email account looks professional. After securing your domain, spend a little more $$$ and purchase the email accounts. #ijs

69

Work for Hire means, "When the party paid to perform the tasks described in the contract has no claim on the ownership of copyright or any related intellectual property rights related to his/her musical performance."

68

The industry keeps evolving. So, should you. READ. READ. READ.*

Don't be afraid to acknowledge unknown people who've inspired you and your creativity. Sometimes you are the only one who places value to a name.

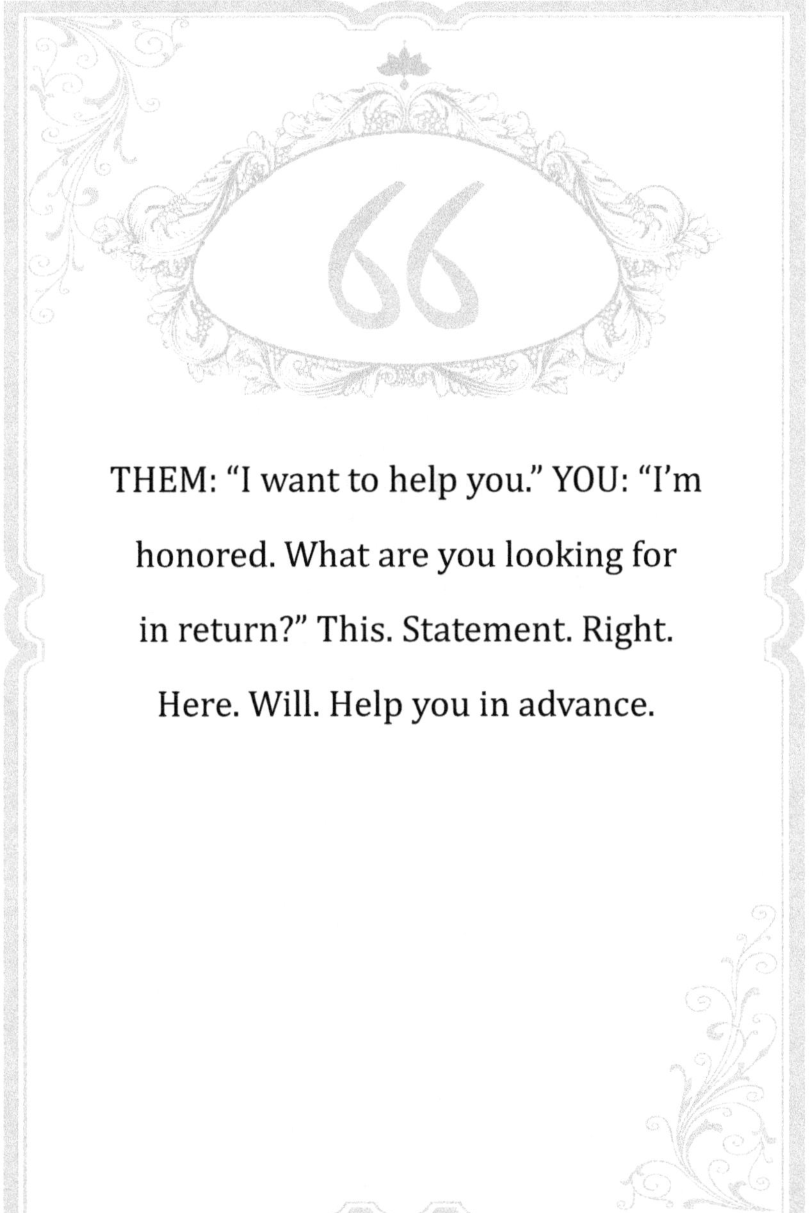

66

THEM: "I want to help you." YOU: "I'm honored. What are you looking for in return?" This. Statement. Right. Here. Will. Help you in advance.

65

Be patient.

64

There's a difference between UPC and ISRC codes. Though they both accurately track your music streams, downloads, merch, Spotify *and other sites*, mechanical royalties and more, the UPC code is a unique identifying code for your album and the ISRCs are used to identify every song.

63

Be prepared to never receive

a returned phone call.

Nothing is FREE.

61

If you can't afford one's services, consider offering gas money and/or a meal. It's called bartering…#ijs

60

Even if you know the answer, ask anyway. Some people want you to remain dumb. Oh, how quickly you will find out who they are. #ijs

59

Remain humble to the day you die.

58

Invest in taking new headshots

or professional photos annually

or at least every two years.

57

Saying THANK YOU goes a long way!

Through Non-Interactive Streaming, aka Internet Radio, listeners play music without the ability to choose the songs that play next. Performance royalties are generated by this form of streaming and are collected through your PRO. Examples: Pandora, Sirius XM, NPR

Interactive Streaming, Services, aka On-demand streaming, services allow listeners to choose the songs that are played. The royalties collected are both Performance and Mechanical. Examples: Spotify, Rdio, Rhapsody, Google Play.

54

If you have the option to opt in and put $ into a 401k, at least invest 5% per paycheck.*

53

As a performing artist, receiving a W-2 eliminates some tax headaches compared to a 1099 artist. A W-2 artist is an employee of an employer who pays you a salary, wage, or other compensation as part of the employment relationship.

52

Congratulations! You have received a few 1099's at the end of the year. But that means the IRS knows how much money you've earned because IT IS TAXABLE INCOME. Roll up those sleeves and grab those receipts. You are considered self - employed.*

51
www.diymusician.cdbaby.com

50

Getting mad at people is not an option

when you know it's a spiritual warfare.

Therefore, address it spiritually

and watch the natural change.

49

Sharing a dressing room with others?

Hygiene...Hygiene...Hygiene.

48

If it can and will benefit others coming after you, pave the way and fight for your rights.

You don't "deserve" anything.

46

It's a sacrifice for a reason.

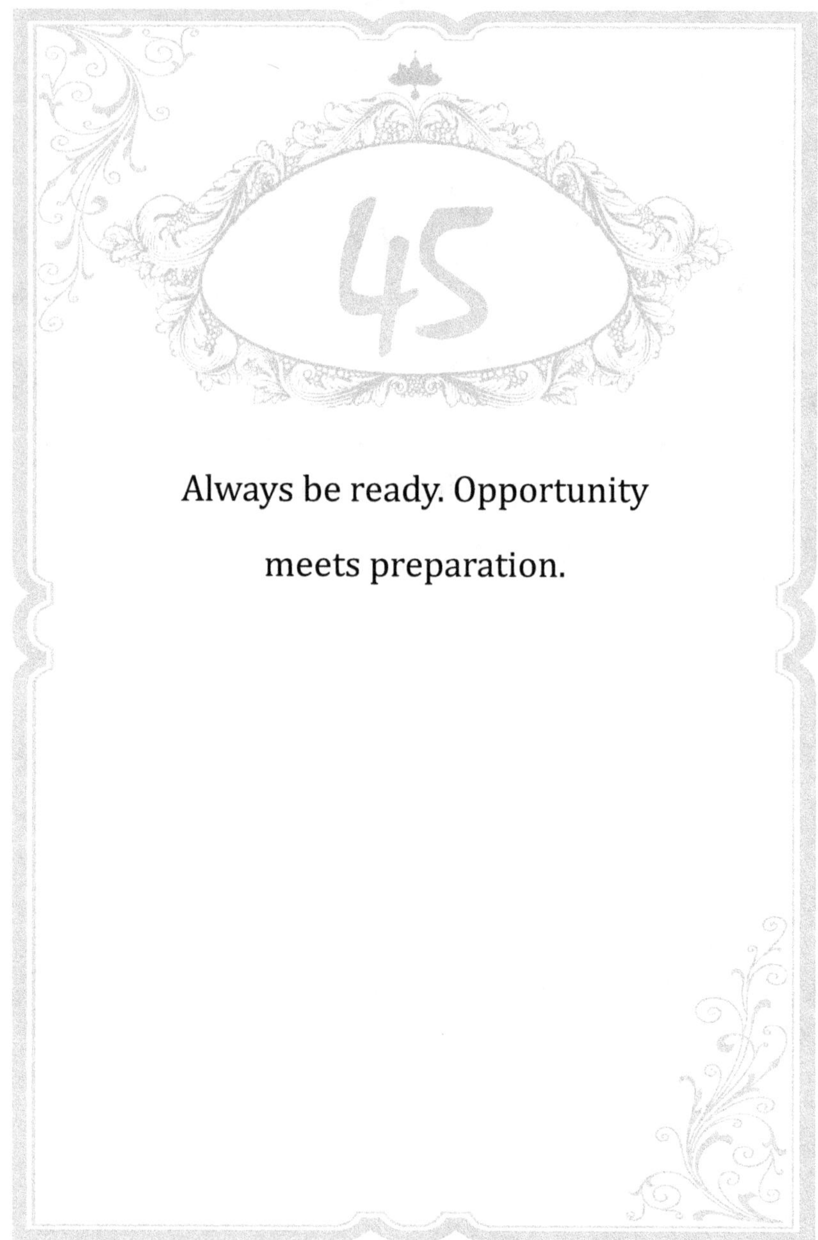

Always be ready. Opportunity

meets preparation.

44

Not all performances pay what you know you are worth. So, make it worthwhile...

43

Resting is just as important as grinding. Find your balance.

Sound Exchange is the sole organization designated by the U.S. Congress to collect and distribute digital performance royalties for sound recordings. It pays featured, non-featured artists, and master rights owners for the non-interactive use of sound recordings under the statutory licenses. www.Soundexchange.com

It hurts when you speak negative of another person as to stop them from advancing. If asked your opinion about a fellow thespian or artist, speak good of them first, then, give an example of an incident that did not fair too good for that person in a previous job. Allow the person asking to make a decision. Don't make it for them.

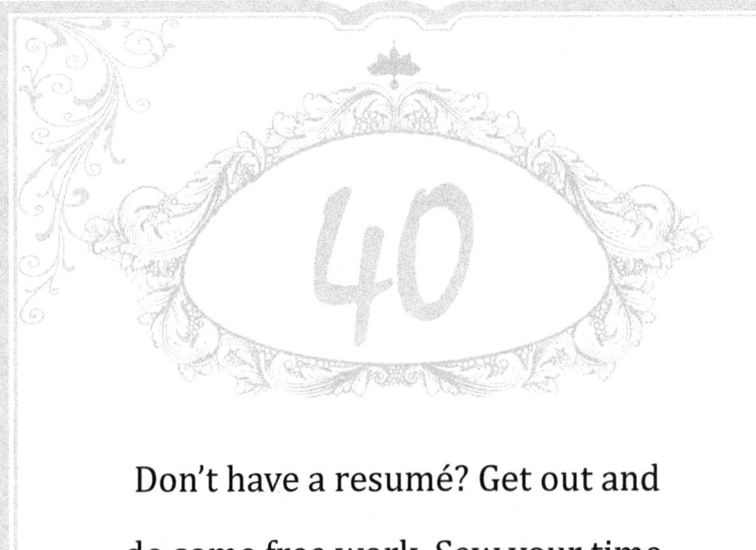

Don't have a resumé? Get out and do some free work. Sew your time. Sew your talent. Learn more by doing and operating in your gift.

39

Ask questions. Don't let pride steal your next job from manifesting.

38

Potpourri Toilet Bowl Spray #ijs

A compulsory mechanical license is a license that the owner of a copyright has to issue. In the U.S., mechanical royalties earned under a compulsory license are paid to the copyright owner on the license at the so-called statutory rate, which is the rate set by the Copyright Board.

36

Find a mentor. Call the mentor. Thank the mentor. Call the mentor. Check on your mentor. Send your mentor cards. Thank the mentor.

35

If people can't answer your questions before you say, "yes" to a performance, for instance, kindly and politely decline the offer.

34

Handling your business can be emotionally draining. My advice: Once you meet someone, get a business card and follow~up within one business day. In your SUBJECT LINE insert: "Nice meeting you."

33

HYDRATE.

32

You can now receive performance royalties from concerts you play. Therefore, submit your list of songs you performed from any concert, gig, or live performance, otherwise known as a "setlist" to your affiliated Performing Rights Organization (P.R.O.). If you perform registered works in venues, bars and restaurants you are entitled these publishing royalties. Submitting your setlists and other performance information allows your P.R.O. to track and pay you the royalties you earn from each live performance.

31

Invest in creating a business plan.

It's a professional vision board.*

30

If someone refers you to an opportunity, the least you can do is call and say, "THANK YOU."

29

Reading from a telephone while performing

is a #negative and un-professional.

28

There's a difference between perception v. reality. Perception, often times, DOES NOT PAY THE BILLS.

27

There are different types of microphones.
Learn which one enhances your sound
and invest in your own. Germs do exist.

26

Don't attend a rehearsal "learning" the music. Know the music ahead of time. It was emailed to you for a reason. You will be surprised how many people don't get called back to an opportunity because of the lack of preparation, respect for the material, and respect for other people's time.

25

When going in for an audition,

dressing the part is always a plus.

Embody the role inside and out.

24

There are benefits to joining Equity,

aka the Actors union. Some are:

Priority access to auditions
Access to better pay
Healthcare
Strict limits on the hours you can be worked

23

Don't get married to a song or track. Some people are good for pulling the plug with the "you owe me" tactics.

22

Don't let your emotions

control your decisions.

21

Sometimes you're next in line

because others quit.

20

Guard your heart and mind at all times.

11

Trust NO ONE.

18

Learn to say, "OK" with no explanations.

17

Trends come and go. But your assignment and purpose will never be outdated. Cherish and build on it. Daily...

16

Invest. In. Yourself.

15

Be on time.

You should always be your own manager, assistant, publicist, agent, lawyer until you have something to manage, publicize, or negotiate. But tread lightly. You may be paying out more than you are receiving.

13

Your gift makes room for you.

12

Prayer changes people and people change things. Are you changing anything?

11

Every and Any-thing is negotiable.

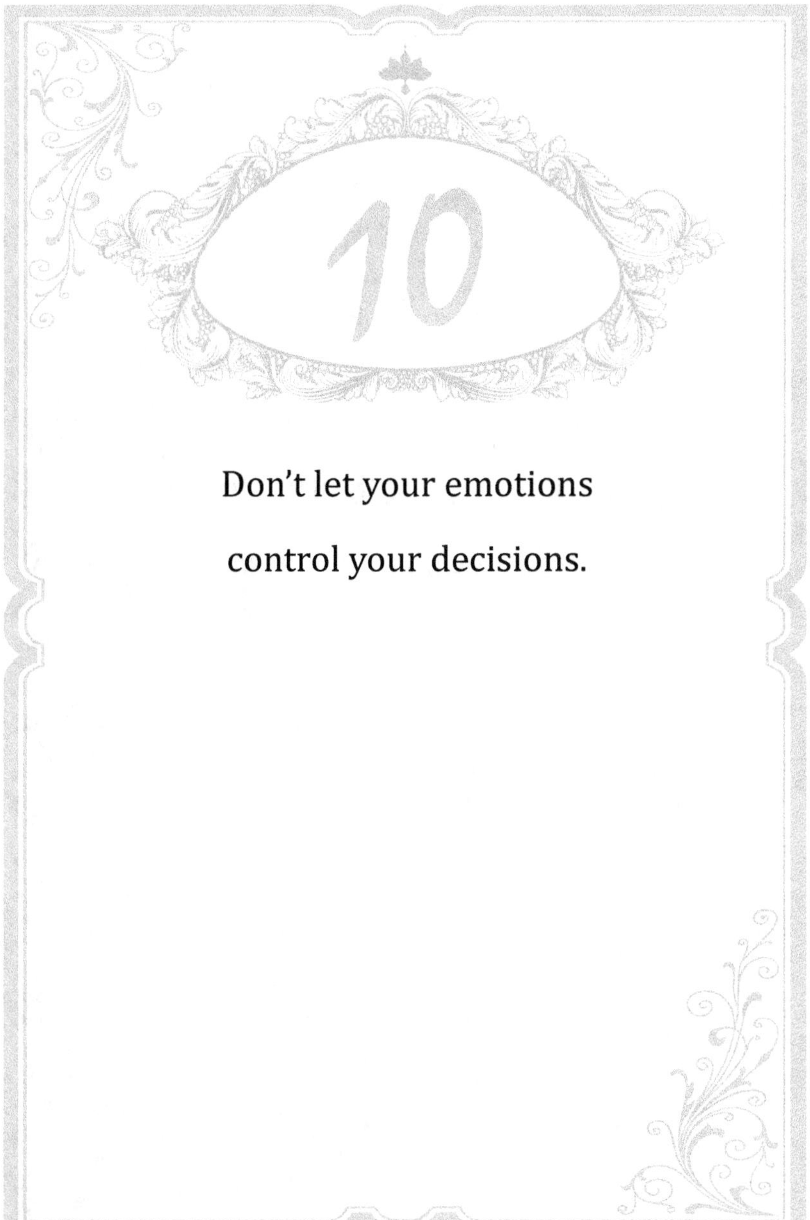

10

Don't let your emotions

control your decisions.

Invest in great lighting for

your video auditions.

Be prepared to HUMBLY walk away.

7

You have every tool and talent you need.

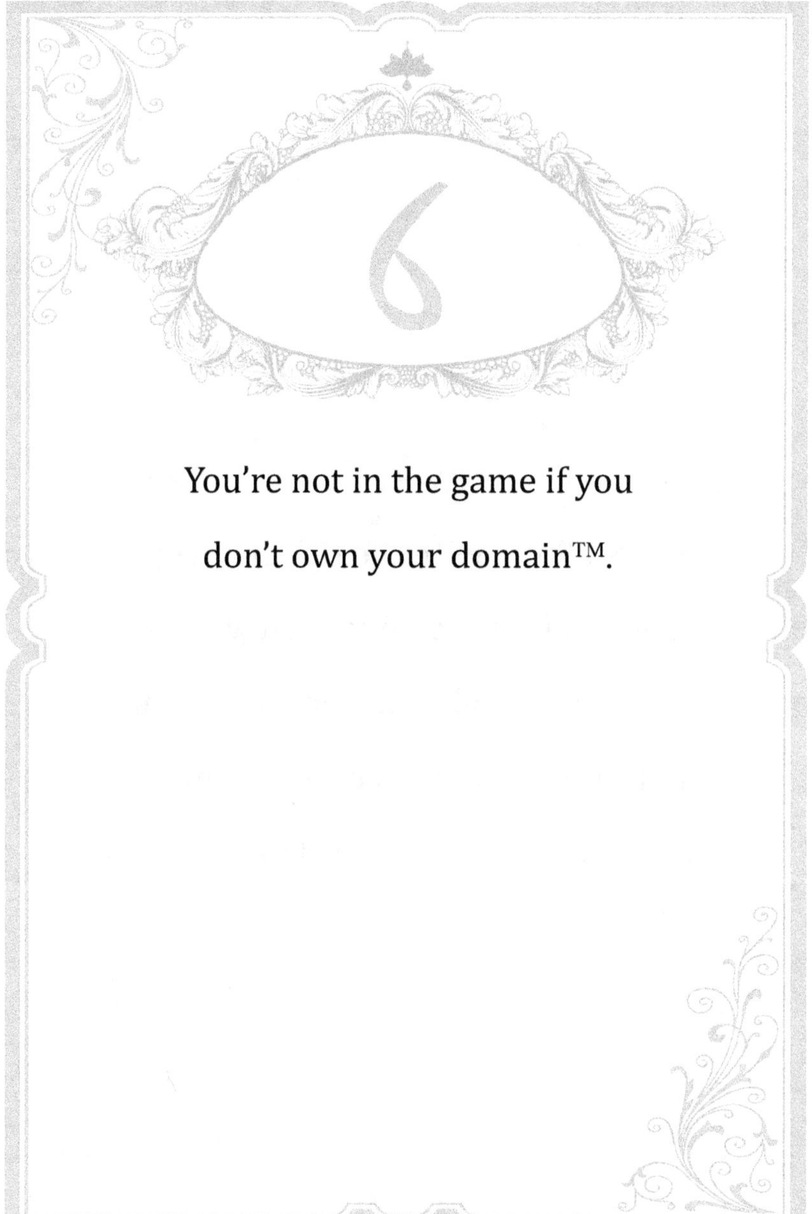

6

You're not in the game if you
don't own your domain™.

You can now register a song or an entire album with the U.S. Copyright Office in minutes through www.Cosynd. com. You can also protect all of your copyrights - your music, videos, images, and documents using this fabulous tool.

4

Perpetuity means "forever." #ijs

FREEDOM is being released

from illegitimate bondage so to

experience becoming what you were

created and redeemed to be.

2

Pray without ceasing.

Jeremiah 9:23 defines SUCCESS ~ "Let not the wise boast of their wisdom or the strong boast of their strength or the rich boast of their riches. But let the one who boasts, boast about this: that they have the understanding to know me, that I am the LORD, who exercises kindness, justice and righteousness on earth, for in these I delight," declares JEHOVAH.